My Bishop and Other Poems

MICHAEL COLLIER

My Bishop and
Other Poems

THE UNIVERSITY OF CHICAGO PRESS
Chicago & London

The University of Chicago Press, Chicago 60637
The University of Chicago Press, Ltd., London
© 2018 by The University of Chicago.
Published 2018
Printed in the United States of America

27 26 25 24 23 22 21 20 19 18   1 2 3 4 5

ISBN-13: 978-0-226-57086-0 (paper)
ISBN-13: 978-0-226-57105-8 (e-book)
DOI: https://doi.org/10.7208/chicago/9780226571058.001.0001

Library of Congress Cataloging-in-Publication Data

Names: Collier, Michael, 1953–
Title: My bishop and other poems / Michael Collier.
Other titles: Phoenix poets.
Description: Chicago ; London : The University of Chicago
    Press, 2018. | Series: Phoenix poets
Identifiers: LCCN 2017056943 | ISBN 9780226570860
    (pbk. : alk. paper) | ISBN 9780226571058 (e-book)
Classification: LCC PS3553.O474645 A6 2018 |
    DDC 813/.54—dc23
LC record available at https://lccn.loc.gov/2017056943

⊗ This paper meets the requirements of ANSI/NISO Z39.48-1992
(Permanence of Paper).

for STANLEY PLUMLY

and ELLEN BRYANT VOIGT

CONTENTS

ACKNOWLEDGMENTS

Many thanks to the editors of the following magazines in which these poems first appeared:

Birmingham Poetry Review (Spring 2017): "My Bishop"

B O D Y (June 30, 2014): "My Father as a Maple Tree" (http://bit. ly/1mcQ7fE)

B O D Y (April 3, 2017): "Meadow" (bodyliterature.com/2017/04/03/ michael-collier-2/)

Cortland Review (Winter 2014): "The Menagerie at Versailles: Haiku from Samuel Johnson's Diary" and "To a Lemon" (http://www.cortlandreview. com/features/14/winter/collier.php#1)

Greensboro Review (2015): "Last Morning with Steve Orlen"

Ibbetson Street 35 (June 2014): "Anecdote of the Piano in the Woods"

Kenyon Review (September / October 2017): "The Storm"

Ploughshares (Spring 2016): "A Wild Tom Turkey"

Plume 43 (February 2015): "To Isabella Franconati" (http://plumepoetry. com/2015/02/to-isabella-franconati/)

The Southampton Review (Summer / Fall 2017), "Koi"

"Bronze Foot in a Glass Case" appeared in *Roads Taken: Contemporary Vermont Poetry*, edited by Sydney Lea and Chard deNiord (Green Writers Press, 2017).

"Jefferson's Bees" appeared in *Monticello in Mind: Fifty Contemporary Poems on Jefferson*, edited by Lisa Russ Spaar (Charlottesville: University of Virginia Press, 2016).

"Last Morning with Steve Orlen" also appeared in Poetry Daily and in *Best*

American Poetry 2016, edited by Edward Hirsch and David Lehman (New York: Scribner's, 2016).

"Len Bias, a Bouquet of Flowers, and Ms. Brooks" appeared in *The Golden Shovel Anthology: New Poems Honoring Gwendolyn Brooks*, edited by Peter Kahn, Ravi Shankar, and Patricia Smith (Little Rock: University of Arkansas Press, 2017).

"A Wild Tom Turkey" also appeared in *Best American Poetry 2017*, edited by Natasha Trethewey and David Lehman (New York: Scribner's, 2017).

Support from the University of Maryland Graduate School was very helpful in completing this collection, as was the support of many friends, including Jennifer Grotz, Edward Hirsch, Jim Longenbach, Sally Keith, David Rivard, Alan Shapiro, and Tom Sleigh. Thanks to Janet Silver for her excellent advice and warm friendship over the years, and to Katherine, Robert, and David.

My Bishop and Other Poems

MEADOW

Moments that were tender—if I can use that word—now rendered in memory's worn face, have names attached and, less vivid, places that are more frequented than present places. Four decades is not so long ago, when facing an open window, hands braced against the sill (moonlight on *her* back) and, outside, grass in furrows, or so it seems to me who's never left for long that window or looked much beyond the meadow and yet have continually wondered what she was looking at, having never, as far as I can see, looked back.

* * *

A WILD TOM TURKEY

When he's in the yard he's hard to find,
not like when he stands in the stubble
across the road brewing his voice

with deeper and deeper percolations
of what sounds like "I'll fuck anything
in feathers," stopping now and then

to display his fan and perform a wobbly
polka, chest heavy as he breasts forward
but never closing on the hens who stay

in wary steps ahead, conversing only
with themselves, their spindly heads foraging,
measuring the distance that frustrates

his occasional flustering leaps so that
when they reach the street, their scurry
provokes him to fly, as if he's both

bull and matador, charging and turning
in the air but landing in a bounding,
rolling heap, which sends a rafter of them

deep into the grass, where after much silence,
what happens sounds like murder.

STRANDS OF HAIR IN A USED BOOK

One light, the other dark
   lie together

(an asymmetrical parenthesis)
   on page 15 of *Green Business*,

by John N. Morris (Atheneum,
   1970)—poems

if read too quickly
   might seem out of fashion,

like these strands of hair
   that are the least evidence

of who the readers were,
   young or old, male or female,

alive now or dead, who,
   perhaps, together or alone,

aloud or silently, had read line 12
   ("What to make of these markings")

as they combed fingers
   through their hair, leaving

behind what the poem leaves,
   an almost

invisible presence.

THREE

1. Awl

As the butt fits
the palm, the elbow
the force, its words
and its work, its
look is its use,
the point of the tool—
leather and wood—
sharp tongue
piercing thought,
stopped and stuck,
a chad of light
punched, not torn.

Stylus minus lead,
you lead by threading
the thread, like reason's
reason, turning right
sends you left, a
needle without eye
upright on your
handyman's bench.

2. Flannery O'Connor & Robert Lowell

"The element of ham in me seeks release."
And that's as the eyes of a peacock fan
look back at you even as the peacock
struts away, picking up each long, rebar-
like leg, such high-stepping, majorette behavior
danced out on those pea-gravel walks, such
beauty, such faith in the cruel miracles
of Lourdes with its piles of canes and crutches
and its unforgiving braces with broken straps.
If you never walked again, if your limbs
stayed disfigured, at least you weren't "inert,
gloomy, aimless, vacant, self-locked," like Lowell,
"a fascinated spirit watching the holocaust
of irrationality, apathy tormenting apathy."

3. The Menagerie at Versailles: Haiku from Samuel Johnson's Diary

The rhinoceros:
skin folds like loose cloth doubled,
big as four oxen.

Camel or dromedary,
both with two bunches,
others with one bunch.

Aviary very large,
the net, black thin wire,
airy and empty.

Cygnets, all tame but restless,
black feet on dark ground.
Halcyons or gulls?

Black stag of China, small.
Lions very tame,
tigers very tame.

The rhinoceros:
yellow horn broken.
The brown bear put out his paws.

JEFFERSON'S BEES

They can cause you a lot of trouble and much pain,
these exotics known by natives as the white man's flies,
but you wouldn't think of it as sorrow or grief,
all that joyful industry they seem to generate,
everyone doing a job, everyone, as my mother
used to say, "at their rank and station." She who had
the orders of angels in mind, she who called
Brazil nuts *nigger toes*—not all the time, though once
was enough to pass that thinking on to me.

—

From his reading he noted Laplanders prepare pine bark
as a substitute for sugar and wondered how far north
bees might live, what routes of migration the harbingers
could survive ahead of the settlements.
No mention of the native *Bombus*, yellow-banded,
scallop-winged, and veined like beveled glass, not heliotropic
like the *Apis* but up and out at dawn, working
to the edge of night, grappling and hugging the stamens—
the flowers sometimes buckling from their weight.

———

If then we can take from our Bees, a considerable
quantity of their superfluous Honey and Wax
without injuring them; if they will work for us
another, and many other Years, and every Year
pay us fair and reasonable Contributions; why
should we treat them *with unnecessary Cruelty*
and hurt Ourselves *by a Greediness, that will turn*
to our Prejudice? No true lover of Bees ever lighted
the fatal Match, that was to destroy his little Innocents.

If you guard them from Accidents, *and save them from Poverty,*
they will continue, by Succession, to the End of the World.
So it is written in "COLLATERAL BEE-BOXES: Or, a New,
Easy, and Advantageous Method of Managing Bees," 1757,
which Edmund Bacon, his overseer, who kept a stand
of more than forty hives, employed, although no records
detailing the perilous, sweet, invasive harvests survive.
Only a sketch shows the boxes near the outhouses,
north and south, adjacent the poultry yards.

———

Two centuries later, they stand east of the house, below
the Loop, almost out of sight, four hives in an enclosure
and two or three more off to the side, less protected,
a little beyond the greenhouses, facing as they should sunrise,
and, like everything at Monticello, restored to an idea
that has not survived its own foreclosures, having been based,
at least in the management of bees, on fostering spring swarms
while suppressing those in late summer, when the blossoming
is over and the workers vie for space with their honey.

EARLY SUMMER

When I put my nose into an open hollyhock or rose
and brush the stamen with the fine hair
that grows along it

and close my eyes to see better what I'm smelling
and filter the pollen through my nostrils
and rub my upper lip beneath the pistils

and inhale the scent's velour of color,
how am I not that collector of essence
who goes from flower to flower,

freighting herself with what she's made to gather,
finding it the way I do by scent and sun
but also by the little dance I've learned,

the waggle of delight my body makes
by clock and compass, that sends me out
into the coming-into-focus garden—

its looming, cavernous attractions,
those blowsy feed bags of silk and plush and velvet
I linger in and do not flit.

TO A LEMON

Hanging from the branches of a neighbor's tree,
you were a vestige of an orchard
where bees returned each spring,
as if the orchard's rows of whitewashed trunks
remained, despite the grids and cul-de-sacs of streets,
a greenish, yellow, knobby goiter,
wrinkled like a forehead and nipple tipped,
waiting to be picked:

mouth on the rind, teeth in the pith,
tongue spritzed by the tart jet
of your tear-shaped cells; zest
on the lips and the wild parrot yellow
of your jacket, pinned with its dark-green stem,
thorn sharp, spit out with pulp and seeds.

LEN BIAS, A BOUQUET OF FLOWERS, AND MS. BROOKS

He arrives in the middle of her reading. She
has to stop and, taking the flowers he's brought, kisses
the beautiful young man whose yellow socks are her
dowdy sweater's antithesis. What's said between them is killed
by applause, but not his smile, which is the smile of a boy
standing in the silence he's created, and
not her magnified stare, which says she
understands why he's arrived late, is
already leaving, and that he is sorry.

EMILY DICKINSON

> *. . . the Horses' Heads*
> *were toward Eternity*

What would she make of the belted cows
that crowd inches from the electrified fence
keeping them from wandering into West Street
and whose heads are the size of junked snowmobiles
they share the pasture with and, if you imagine
ears as handlebars, even a little shaped
like them—their nostrils snorting
the white-blue exhaust of gasoline?

As they wrap their tongues around grass
and weeds along the road, swallowing
whole the braided, green hanks a hand
can't rip, you see how their steady rumination
and the slow two-man reciprocating saw
of mandibles appears eternal, but it's not.
Eternity is the great, deep nothing, the warm,
watery blankness in their eyes that you see
when they lift their heads, not to look at you
but to make easier their endless need to swallow.

KOI

Following a path that followed the sloping
contour of the land, through a break in a wall
that seemed built only to hold espaliered vines
and trees, trunks corkscrewed
near the ground but straightening
as they rose, their branches handcuffed,

and then beyond a second wall,
a third terrace, we found it *where the strangers*
said we would, larger than a backyard swimming pool
but shallower, filled with murk,
a clotted, darkly shaded surface beneath which moved
tubular leviathans, yes, leviathans, bow-headed—

orange, gold, red and black, white-flecked—
nudging toward us like a crowd of souls.
No one was there to say how much
of the pellets to sow, only
a neatly printed sign: KOI FOOD
with an unnecessary arrow aimed at

a plastic bucket with a clear top, hard to unsnap,
that made a starting pistol's crack
and sent the koi in a counterclockwise churn.
But it was not until we cast handfuls
in careless, strafing arcs that they thrashed and roiled,
tails and fins breaching water, white and turbid,

a ferocity that ceased as quickly as it began,
    and though we cast out more,
they turned away: lumbering, disinterested, unschooled,
    moving fluidly, impossibly avoiding contact. And so
they came to rest not without motion
    but anchored like a fleet.

*　*　*

BOOM BOOM

I leave my backyard and enter the alley in search of my poetry. I get lost a few houses down near the Eldridges' because all the fences and trash cans are identical. I am alone filling a shirt pocket with the bees David Hills eviscerates by pulling out their stingers and that he has lined up on a flap torn from a cardboard box that's pinned to the ground with four small stones. In a toolbox I have a small hammer and screwdrivers for taking things apart. Above me is the sky that is always blue. (This means at night the stars are what I see but can't count.) The alley is dirt. My shoes scuff its uneven surface. Suddenly a door opens, a dog barks, it is Boom Boom, a Chihuahua, not even a dog in my mind. It rushes its side of the fence and is so much louder and fiercer than it needs to be. After a while it stops. Now it sounds like a tambourine because of a collar with tiny bells. Passionflowers grow in a thick vine over Boom Boom's fence. I have been told the leaves of these flowers are the lances that pierced Jesus's chest and broke his legs. Boom Boom is whimpering, lying down near a place in the fence through which I squeeze my hand to touch his nose. "Boom Boom," I say, very quietly, "I love you. You are the only one who understands me." Afterwards, I feel very small and very large, restrained and freed, and certain there is a purpose to life beyond the one I've been given.

MY BISHOP ✶

The summer of high school graduation I felt God was calling me to the priesthood.

What I mean by "calling" is not that he spoke to me in a language I understood but that he had given me access to immense and ecstatic experiences of love and joy, not real experiences but ones I perceived as if a limitless future was inside me, as if, and this is why it seemed like a "calling," I

was being invited to see the world that lay behind and beyond the one we are born into.

I began to kneel in my bedroom and pray, not prayers I had been taught but rather ones that inhabited me and for which I was their instrument.

Sometimes as I prayed the sun would come down out of the sky and compress into a flower.

Sometimes people I did not know materialized in the room and prayed with me, and how glad and comforted I was by that intimacy.

Sometimes the prayers were like violent caresses and I would masturbate.

I was eighteen and wanting to live a life filled with meaning, I wrote one of my Jesuit High School teachers about entering the Order.

What he told me was that I should listen not to the voice coming from inside me or the voice from the world beyond but I should listen to the voice coming from the physical world.

He said, God is immanent, everywhere, open, and available.

———

Bishop, my first thought when I saw you enter the funeral home chapel for my
father's Rosary was that you peroxide your hair and then as you came
nearer how little changed by time your face seemed, except for a single
bangle of a double chin, but no age lines, no grotesque enlargement of

ears and nose, just a smooth, worriless, mild, unreadable, Irish counte-
nance and that gingery hair, incongruous in a man so plain.

A fondness for you stirred in me not as a kind of pity for what you'd become
but for what I realized you'd always been: a short, insecure man with a
compassionate heart, proficient at following directions but lacking the
common touch—and whose timidity was now a form of cowardice?

——

What a beautiful detail, what a fine recollection to nudge me with in front of
my father's coffin—that you watched the *Smothers Brothers* for the
first time when my parents invited you for a Sunday dinner.

Was remembering that show a way of getting a conversation going after forty
years, a quick nod to something we'd shared and then on to the real
subject?

And what would that have been, the real subject?

What I remember is that you let my father celebrate alone the sacrament of
cocktail hour, the way he did most nights: on the counter a bar towel
folded just so on which to rest a long, small stirring spoon, its handle
topped with a ceramic cherry.

Drink in hand, paper coaster at the ready, he'd watch the news, while from the
hallway a gilt-framed, papal marriage blessing with its holy-card cameo
of Pius XII admonished him.

In our house nothing was done without the Pope looking on, like the time
semi–*in flagrante* on the living-room floor with a girl I looked up and
there he was, *Papa*, in his white *zucchetto*.

—

For your episcopal motto you chose "To Build Up the Body of Christ," apt for
the once young, friendly priest and team chaplain who lifted weights
at the Universal Gym next to the K-Mart on West Indian School Road,
who never stopped reminding us to play fair, who even in his cassock

could dribble, fake, and set a shot, or spiral a football, and whose wry,
almost cheerful expression met us in the sacristy when, as Knights of
the Altar, we'd flip on the white row of switches that lighted up the
church, flooding the dark processionary of the nave, reflecting off the

cold floor of polished stone like the bottom of a stream, a fine relief
of gray blue, gravel and pebbles—the light all at once expelling the
shadows, the vacant spaces that left me calm, certain of purpose, as I
filled cruets with wine and water, slipping the folded, starched

purificator between the crystal vessels on their glass tray, while you
vested, whispering in Latin: "Gird me, O Lord, with the cincture of
purity, and quench in my heart the fire of concupiscence, that the
virtue of continence and chastity may abide in me."

So many snippets of prayers, spells of liturgy, Latin and English, parables and
miracles—the coal we lit to burn the incense; the clang of the chain
against the thurible; bowing, genuflecting, crossing ourselves—all of
it abides in me still, serene now, vivid in the radiance of my disbelief.

——

And while the fire in your heart had been quenched, it was not so for the other
assistant pastor, Robert B. Gluch, who had charge of the Knights.

Twenty-eight of us in cassocks and surplices, hands steepled as we stood tiered
on the altar steps, Gluch not quite in the center at the back, taller by a
head, and wearing an ornate cape with a clasp.

Four of us with closed eyes, six of us smirking, including myself.

McDonogh and Braun eyeless behind the reflected glare on their spectacles.

Gluch beatific, head tilted, a male Mary.

———

When my mother saw my father laid out in his rented casket, she asked, in her deaf-person's loud *sotto voce*, "Who did that to Bob?" And then, "He looks awful!"

And yet, Bishop, for you she was all false kindness.

"How did you find us?" she wanted to know, as if your presence was both mystery and miracle, and then through the cloud of her dementia, she asked it again, then again and again.

And so, with my mother perseverating and with the waxworks version of my father behind us, and my wife and children, my sisters, brothers-in-law, nephews and nieces, my parents' nona- and octogenarian friends, my dearest childhood friends gathered all around . . . you turned from

her, as if she wasn't speaking, to ask if I was "right with the church," and then because "it would please your father," you offered to hear my confession, whenever I was ready.

———

Pacing back and forth between the white-lined spaces of the parish parking lot, holding his breviary in front of him like a dowser, Gluch would recite his daily offices, and like a land shark, when his head turned his body followed.

Once, as I was cutting through the playground to avoid him, he caught my eye and waved me over.

In what must have seemed play to others, he put his arms around me and quickly—my hands becoming feet, my feet in their shoes beneath his chin—turned me upside down.

"I hear you're spreading rumors, Collier."

"You better not."

"You better goddamn not."

And then he swung me like a pendulum.

—

In his letter to Can Grande, Dante describes the meaning of the *Divine Comedy* as not only the state of souls after death but also God's justice as it's manifested in those souls.

Paolo and Francesca forever buffeted by the storm of their lust are caught up in a whirlwind that brings them together, even as it sends them apart.

Can Grande was Dante's benefactor. His name means "Big Dog."

Like you he was an eminence but unlike you he was loved *and* feared.

—

Of course, I wasn't "right" with the church.

But then as if I needed to convince you I was a good man who had lived an ethical life, I introduced you to my wife and sons.

Did that give you a larger opening into my soul?

Is that why you offered to hear my confession, as if you knew it was only a matter of time before I'd come to recognize the need for a particular kind of repentance?

———

All those priests you moved unbeknownst from parish to parish, I see them
in Hell, wearing their genitals around their necks instead of the white
collars of their office, and the darkness, at least in this circle, is the dark
of a black light in which certain textures irradiate a violet shimmer.

In this atmosphere you see what they wear before you see them. By "you" I
mean you, Bishop, for having shielded them in life, I've put you in
their eternal fraternity.

And where might you put me?

In the narrow, deep crack between belief and disbelief, with those who keep
their heads above its chasm by spreading out their arms so their bodies
dangle in the emptiness between?

———

I couldn't agree more, Bishop, no one wants to hear a description of human genitals.

The first adult penis I saw was my father's, flaccid, hanging from him as he shaved, right at the level of my face, like three pieces of unfamiliar fruit, the one in the center peeled, free of its hairy rind, the end of which smooth and purplish was similar to mine but so much bigger it

imposed on me an image of what my body might become, gargantuan, foreign, and accompanied by terrifying demands.

—

What I feared about Gluch was that he knew something about me I didn't know and that's why when he called my mother with an invitation for me to go overnight with him to the Grand Canyon, although she'd already consented, I refused.

But more powerful than the fear of what he might have known about me was the fear that if I went with him, I'd be forever on the other side of my life, even if he didn't fondle me or suck my dick, and I was afraid, too, shame would come between the admiration I had for you, Bishop,

and the loyalty that went with it.

I refused, I refused, I refused.

How easily he had turned my mother into my betrayer.

For decades this event was like a dark black space between her and me.

Several years ago, as I was watching the evening news with her, your face rose up from the depths of the screen, like an image in a Magic 8 Ball.

In her habit of talking to the TV, she asked, "What do they do to those boys?"

"Oral sex, Mom," I said, "oral sex."

—

My father needed a presentable shirt for his viewing so I went to Sears the day
before and took a long time deciding if I should buy the fifteen-dollar
polyester-cotton blend or spend five more for the all-cotton.

———

The girl I was making out with under Pius XII's watchful eye—if she had pleaded with me to stop, to get off her, "now," if she'd pushed me away, would I?

———

Creeping up from behind us in the sacristy, Gluch enfolded me and another
server, as we were called, inside his chasuble, and mimicking Count
Dracula invited us to come into his castle where he would show us
something.

In a fake, cowering voice, the other boy said, "What are you going to show us
father?" and then we both slipped out from beneath his arms.

I had been silent, wary, uncertain of what to do, and yet the other server knew
in an instant how to make a joke of it and escape.

And yet both of us had been under his wing, so to speak—altar boy to priest,
servant to master, sheep to shepherd, penitent to confessor.

Later, when I was carrying the cruets of wine and water out to the sanctuary,
the hem of my cassock made a brisk sibilance as it brushed the tops of
my shoes, a sound like a voice that said, as I hear it now, "Tenderness
is in us all."

———

Last night, I was on a train, sitting at a table in the dining car with my friend Tom.

I was wearing a black cassock, unbuttoned along its length, collarless.

When you appeared, your cassock buttoned, collar hidden, except for the tooth-sized tab at the front, Tom and I were talking.

Around your neck hung a cross, decorated with inlaid turquoise.

How odd, I thought, that you've found me attired like this, in a dream, posing as a cleric.

I explained to Tom that you had been like a father to me—no pun intended— and how your hands on my shoulders once steadied me, as well as another acolyte, before the three of us exited the sacristy, crossed the sanctuary, and processed down the aisle to the vestibule to meet a

mother, father, and infant in their coffins.

And then with some sadness and apropos of what I don't know I opened a briefcase, took out a newspaper—the *New York Times*, June 17, 2003— and read: "Beleaguered by a sexual misconduct scandal involving clergy, [the bishop of Phoenix] was arrested Monday in connection

with a fatal hit-and-run accident. . . . he was driving the car Saturday and thought he hit a dog or cat or someone threw a rock. . . . the bishop made phone inquiries about replacing his damaged windshield before police confronted him."

Tom wanted to know if you were the pedophile I'd told so many stories about over the years.

"No, this is the good priest," I said. "The one who became Bishop."

Then Tom wanted to know if Gluch had ever molested me.

Before I could respond, I saw that you were crying.

Not because I wanted to but because it's what's done, I put my arm around you.

"If you thought it was a dog or cat, why didn't you stop?" Tom asked.

"I'm not crying for the dog," you said, impatiently.

"I'm crying because Gluch was a good priest."

———

In Gluch's obituary parishioners at Saint Odelia's, his last posting before he died, remembered him with great fondness.

Perhaps that's all we can hope for, to be remembered with fondness.

——

I meant to say that when your face appeared on the television, my mother first remarked, "He's not a bright man," and then I told her what was done to those boys.

———

When my father was an altar boy, he had a bishop who gave him (this was the Depression) a dollar or two, sometimes a five, after serving Mass, meant not for him, it was understood, but for his family who'd "lost everything," as the phrase goes.

In my father's version of the story, his bishop performed an act of charity that allowed my father to save face and required nothing from him but trust.

———

In my version of the story, well, Bishop, why don't you tell me what happens in my version of the story?

———

Fondness aside, when you showed up at the funeral home, I realized how much I disliked you, which surprised me, and not even the grief I felt for my father could forgive it.

I thought to myself, Why do you think you can just show up here?

Who do you think you are?

———

In my version of the story, four years pass and my Bishop shows up at my
mother's funeral.

He's pushing a walker with squeaky, plastic wheels and fluorescent tennis balls
fixed to the back legs.

His face is slack.

A white pharmaceutical rime crusts the corners of his mouth.

His gingery hair is gray.

I follow his slow effort to reach the altar where he presumes he's wanted as a
concelebrant but no one has invited him.

At first he won't look at me directly, but when our eyes meet, he administers
a fierce, unforgiving stare.

He sees I'll never be ready for confession.

I pity him.

It's what we do.

I pity, dislike, and I'm fond of him.

The truth of this is almost as bearable as the lie.

Later, when I approach the sanctuary to deliver my mother's eulogy, I give
him a quick, involuntary wave like a signal of surrender or a sign that
recognizes who we were more than forty years ago—frightened boy
and less frightened young priest.

From the lectern, before I begin, I thank him publicly for his friendship.

ANECDOTE OF THE PIANO IN THE WOODS

I came upon a piano in the woods.
Its silver casters balanced on three stones.
A harp lay inside the lean-to of its top.

No bench, except the air, which meant
its silence roused the trees.
The leaves were the music's million,

million ears. The limbs, a hundred
thousand raised batons. Pollen was
yellow snow on its lacquered skin.

Like a swinging bridge above a flooded
creek the keys were rippling dominoes,
and the water running beneath,

molded to the shape of stones below,
was an always moving, never changing
melody, a surface score whose swells

and hollows, whose shadows, read
by sight, sounded a chorus of a single note,
that sounded like a piano in the woods.

———

＊ ＊ ＊

VITALIS

The bottle stood in my father's medicine cabinet, square-shouldered, narrowing to a waist, like the torso of a fullback. You could grip it with one hand and with the other twist the red, grooved top, shake a few oily drops into your palm, and, having already put the cap and bottle down, rub the dressing between your hands to spread it evenly through your hair. Even on weekends, a towel around his waist, he faced the fogged-up mirror. That's how men once stood at their ablutions, that's how my father, captain of salesmen at William Volker, put his game face on. Not like a Spartan oiling his hair before battle, but lathering up with Burma Shave, tightening the blade in the razor, and pulling with sure strokes through stubble so stiff you could hear the emery friction, and then the one-two, one-two slap with Old Spice as if he were his own sparring partner, feinting and jabbing, bobbing and weaving, ready again to take himself on, believing he'd sell better than he'd been sold, like this day and the next, walking out the door, change jingling in his pockets, a money clip pinching its bills.

THE STORM

Our landlord, a federal bureaucrat, would sit in his car
across the street at the end of the month to collect rent.
He had a scarlet birthmark covering his neck
and tinting the lobe of his left ear. That's what
you got for a $125 a month on Capitol Hill
in 1981, a landlord afraid to enter his own building
and a three-hundred-square-foot "garden" apartment.

I did odd jobs for him, painting the long, dark
brick passageway that went past our door,
into the concrete yard and unpaved eeriness of the alley,
and twice repaired locks on apartments upstairs
that had been burglarized. One victim, a newly divorced
woman in her midthirties who lived above us, broke her lease
and moved out. She had dark hair in a style more suitable
for someone much older, combed over on top to disguise a thin spot.
In my mother's parlance, she seemed "ill-equipped to deal with life."

When I called the landlord to say she had "vacated the premises,"
a phrase that came out of my mouth involuntarily, he was silent
for several seconds before calling her a "fuck."
I thought she'd done the right thing considering how
shaken she was and that, among other things, as I was installing
a dead bolt, she said it felt as if she'd been raped, actually,
she used the phrase "gang raped," which seemed hyperbole
to me until I told my wife who without pausing said of course
that's what you'd feel if you were a woman.

Night or day it was the kind of neighborhood
where if something happened you couldn't trust someone
to come to your aid, like the evening my wife and I
were fixing dinner and heard over the radio's drone,
or perhaps through it, what sounded like shouts and screams
or cries; all three, I guess. Beyond the window we could see
a woman flailing, on her side in the street. By the time I reached her
she was up and pointing down the block to a figure running away.
Instinct of a kind I'd never felt sent me after the man
but only the distance of a house or two until another more familiar instinct
sent me back to the woman who was now rubbing the side of her face,
and from instinct, too, I put my arm around her and then,
I don't know how else to say it, she "buried" her face in my shoulder.
"I'm sorry," she said. "I'm so sorry."

———

When one of my sons turned twenty-five, I calculated how old
I would be when he turned fifty, if I were still alive, and then
it occurred to me that after I die his age will begin
to catch up to mine, until at some point in the future,
if he lives long enough, we will for one year
be the same age, the only time in our lives, so to speak,
when I am not keeping ahead of him moving toward death
and he has not yet surpassed me, and in order for me to experience
what he will experience that day, I will have to live until
I'm a month shy of ninety-six, which is how long my father lived.

———

The afternoon the Air Florida jet crashed in the Potomac
I was working in the basement apartment on Tenth Street.
The blizzard had been accompanied by lightning and thunder,
big booms and flashes, as if there were a storm within a storm.

By noon the schoolyard across the street had close to a foot.
One of the many times I got up from my work to look out
the small window, I saw a group of boys tramping slowly
in a jagged file across the playground, each carrying a large

household item: a TV with its cord dragging, a turntable atop
an amplifier, speakers, an IBM typewriter. The last boy dragged
a red plastic sled with a bulky, olive-green duffel bag as freight.
"Looters in the Snow," I thought, like a Bruegel painting.

We lived close enough to National to hear planes land
and take off, intermittent muffled rumblings I'd learned
to ignore, although at first I tracked them tensely
like a passenger strapped in his seat silently urging the plane up.

Back then, I was afraid of so many things. I dealt with fear
by acting brave and impervious, cultivating as well
an ironic bonhomie that covered up the effort.
Everything was an effort, so I made effortlessness my goal.

At night, what I'd avoided during the day appeared
in the form of my child self: a pale, chubby, asthmatic boy
brought too easily to tears, who could not say no for cowardice
the time at the state fair he rode "The Hammer" with an older boy he admired.

Rising in the gondola above the midway with its tantalizing lights,
he felt alive in a peculiar but appealing way as it rocked gently.
For a moment courage was like gaining altitude incrementally
and yet, from having waited his turn in line, he knew what was coming.

If you want to know what fear looks like, look at the boy
when he finishes the ride. He's smiling because he thinks
everyone is watching him, and that's why, too, when his friend suggests
they ride again he keeps smiling and can't believe what he's agreed to do.

———

Along with the hospice nurse, who kept increasing his morphine,
reassuring me she had the orders for upping the dose,
which meant she was hastening his departure, I was with my father when he died.
And yet the nurse, whose name I can't remember, although
I promised myself never to forget, had been trying hard to keep him alive.
She brought out a nebulizer to help him breathe.
"Robert, cough. Cough, Robert," she urged.
He hadn't responded to either of us for several hours, yet we could
hear him struggling to comply or maybe he was trying to speak.
No matter, a few hours later the nurse told me quietly he was near the end
and if family wanted to see him before he passed I should let them know.
What took them so long getting there I didn't ask.
The nurse stayed with us, meaning my father and me, as I kept waiting
for my sisters and brothers-in-law to come through the door or kept hoping
they wouldn't so I would have the moment to myself, not to myself
but for myself, with my father, whose ragged breathing, occasional gasps,
and, yes, coughing, had become thin and shallow, although his fingers roved
over the sheet and even jumped now and then. His head at an angle
on the pillow made it seem as if he was concentrating
extremely hard on the ceiling as if, I thought, he was listening
to someone talking to him from up there and all the effort
he had been expending hour after hour to catch his breath, to let
go of the great sighing his lungs and mouth produced, the heaves
and groans, the agitated restlessness of his body, the unappeasable
shiftings of his discomfort, had left him washed-up, alone
and isolated as the tide, which had been ebbing all night and into
the morning was so far out and had taken with it so much
shore that my father was left on a pedestal of sand, around
which a shallow moat dissipated the further the tide withdrew,
and just as I in my exhaustion believed he was the island
of Mont-Saint-Michel—his head the cathedral nestled in the tightly
clustered village, his nose the spire rising from the bell tower—
just then his utterly blue eyes opened. Shocked by their own awakening
they looked at whatever it was they saw, which is why when his eyes

closed and he died, his mouth remained open. The last thing the nurse did was to brush, no, to flick his hair up off his forehead.

—

The plane's tail hit the Fourteenth Street bridge, sheared open automobiles
stalled in the storm-clogged traffic, and then went nose first
into the frozen river. Twenty years later, the sister
of one of the crash victims said, "There's a tenacity

the dead have on the living that no living person has on you."
When the rescue helicopter got low enough over the Potomac
the pilot could see through the whiteout a few people standing
on one of the jet's wings. To say the river was frozen

isn't really accurate. It was chockablock with ice floes.
The plane had opened up a lead in the ice between it
and the shore that was covered quickly with jet fuel.

—

For part of the war my father was stationed in DC as a flight controller
at National. Late one night, he guided Charles Lindbergh to a landing
and then went on the field to meet him. Since Lindbergh
was there only to refuel, they walked among the planes, talking.

For many years, my father carried in his billfold a dollar
Lindbergh had signed and given to him. He called it a "short snorter."
This meant if he ever met Lindbergh again and couldn't produce the bill,
he'd have to buy him a drink.

When he was first assigned to National, my father lived alone
in an apartment that would eventually house my mother and oldest sister
who were then with family in Indianapolis. One night awakened
by a tapping at the window, he hauled up the blinds to find

a man's legs and feet dangling from above. On the few occasions
I heard him tell this story, he provided little more than
what I've written here. I never thought to ask him, as I'd like to now,
what effect discovering that man had on his life.

I'd like to know, too, if he ever thought about killing himself.
A day rarely passes without my college roommate,
Jimmy O'Laughlin, who asphyxiated himself in his father's car,
coming into my thoughts or appearing in his bell-bottoms

and flowery shirts, hair teased and ratted like Rod Stewart's
and his side of the room littered with crushed packs of KOOLs
and discarded cups of Laura Scudder vanilla pudding,
which he used to snuff out the butts. What might it mean

that during the semester O'Laughlin began to contemplate his demise,
I was writing an art history paper on Dadaist suicide.
Dada was like throwing a full garbage can into someone's backyard
or swimming pool, something I did with friends in high school.

We called it "alley aping." And Dada suicide was an act of such
nonchalance and indifference that I mistook it for courage.
When Giacometti was asked, "Have you ever thought of suicide?"
he replied, "I think of it every day, but not because I find life intolerable,

not at all, rather because I think death must be a fascinating
experience." That's not how I think of suicide. I think of it
as one among many solutions to the problem of living,
different than the others, all of which involve staying alive.

Freud said it is impossible to imagine our own deaths,
he who imagined his down to its exact dosage in morphine.
When O'Laughlin climbed inside his father's car
and started it up in the garage, he had moved home to finish

two incompletes so he could graduate with our class,
that was his particular problem of living.

———

Twenty years ago, when I first wrote about the crash,
I began, "So, you were in a cave of your own making."
Meaning the three hundred square feet of apartment where,
after my wife left for work, I rolled up the foam mat

we slept on, brought a chair in from the other room,
and worked at a narrow, plywood desk, a desk lamp
the only light, warm and intimate, but intense
and clarifying for the way it invited concentration.

And then I wrote: "You got up from the desk
And walked to the window covered by security bars."
That's when I saw the boys crossing the playground.
My first thought was "Looters in the Snow" because

I'd been memorizing John Berryman's "Winter Landscape,"
which is based on Bruegel's *The Hunters in the Snow.*
As I looked through the bars at the freezing world,
what should have been a quiet scene shook with thunder

and was lit up with clouds that pulsed with lightning.
I recited the poem silently, slowly, and imperfectly,
as if I were lip-synching sounds I heard in my head.
Sometimes I repeated the previous line to get to the next.

Here's the middle of the poem:

> Are not aware that in the sandy time
> To come, the evil waste of history
> Outstretched, they will be seen upon the brow
> Of that same hill: when all their company
> Will have been irrecoverably lost,

These men, this particular three in brown
Witnessed by birds will keep the scene . . .

———

The woman who had been mugged had written her
phone number and name on a scrap of paper I had torn
from a yellow legal pad I used for writing, and for several months
I kept it folded in my wallet. If I called her I'd be setting

in motion events beyond my control, which is what
I must have wanted, but not enough. Occasionally, I'd take it out.
It reminded me of how when I put my arm around her
I also brushed away her hair from her face with my fingers

and curled it behind her ear to stay in place.

———

The mnemonic that recalls the address of the Capitol Hill apartment
behind the Marine barracks on Eighth Street, SE, that billeted
the drum and bugle corps and honor guards for state functions
the year my wife and I lived in DC (747 Tenth Street) is *Jumbo Jet*.
Four stories of watery-green brick, tallest on a block that marked
the edge of a neighborhood's stalled gentrification. Fall into early spring
on Friday nights we could hear the sounds of the bands fade in and out
as if on a tide. Cannons going off ricocheted inside the parade ground,
announced the ceremony's end. Our windows hummed, and once
a small jade horse stationed on a shelf fell over and broke a hoof.
The bands were called the Commandant's Own and the President's Own.

—

O'Laughlin was in Yale Psychiatric Institute recovering from
an earlier suicide attempt when on Tuesday, October 13, 1970,
the day Bobby Seale was appearing in New Haven for a pretrial
hearing as the accused for the murder of a fellow Black Panther,
O'Laughlin phoned in a bomb threat but didn't specify
why or where so the police evacuated three courthouses.

At our tenth college reunion I said to Betty, his
former girlfriend, that if Jimmy had only known
how much he was loved . . . "Are you kidding," she said.
"Give me a fucking break. He knew he was loved."

———

One night, a few days after the crash, I was driving back
from a party, late, alone, on the George Washington Parkway,
which because of high-banked snow was like a shallow,
roofless tunnel. Headlights reflected off the opposite side

of the road as I came into a turn, a blue-white, arctic
shimmer and as such the dark, clear night above pressed down,
or so it seemed, as if it had physical weight, but when the road
made a wide, broad turn, and with the shoulders plowed

on either side flush to the pavement, the river came into view
and across it the dome of the Jefferson. Up ahead, brighter
than day, towers of high-intensity floodlights lit up
the near end of the bridge. Suspended in the illumination,

rising by cable up a crane and dripping with water, was the tail
of the plane, growing larger but stranger as I drew closer.
Stranger because it was exactly what it appeared to be, or I should say
what I expected it to be, but at the same time it was larger,

monumental, a warrior's shield inscribed with a runelike logo,
a Celtic or Arabic intertwining riddle, an empire's seal,
so much shaped metal, trapezoidal, hanging, twisting
as it came to a stop. But it wasn't until I was heading

into the District on the undamaged span that it became fully
what it was, torn off its body, a wounded appendage, an explosion
of peeled-back skin, bone and tendon and arteries severed, distended,
and no mnemonic or involuntary phrase to repair or rename what it was,

not a link in the chain of modern disasters, not a harbinger of wrecks
and salvages—the unceasing drone of cranes and claws loading barges
with misshapen beams and miles of wire and glass that didn't melt—
but a scrap of paper with a name, a power cord dragging in snow,

O'Laughlin hanging up the phone, my father's short snorter,
a bit boring through the door, the airplane picking up speed,
thunder inside of snow, "God, look at that thing,"
one of the pilots said, "that don't look right."

MY FATHER AS A MAPLE TREE

As large as a one-
footed elephant,
its several trunks

and tusks
bent landward, leafed
and petaled.

And in its hundred, two
hundred years of age,
bowed not by kneeling

on that leg
but by the troubling
weight of wind

and its own heavy,
splintered crown,
while a great palmetto ear,

like a burned-out sponge,
lay on the ground.
That's how he looked

this morning—
a thrashing, fissured
monument pecked

by birds that nominate
his skin, a boundary
tree, cleaved

by lightning, lost
to what it bound.

"Jesus Christ,"
a neighbor urged,
"cut it down."

LAST MORNING WITH STEVE ORLEN

"Last night I wrote a Russian novel or maybe it was English.
Either way, it was long and boring. My wife's laughter
might tell you which it was, and when she stops,
when she's not laughing, let's talk about the plot
and its many colors. The blue that hovered in the door
where the lovers held each other but didn't kiss.
The red that by mistake rose in the sky with the moon,
and the moon-colored sun that wouldn't leave the sky.
All night I kept writing it down, each word arranged
in my mouth, but now, as you can see, I'm flirting
with my wife. I'm making her laugh. She's twenty.
I'm twenty-five, just as we were when we met, just
as we have always been, except for last night's novel,
Russian or English, with its shimmering curtain of color,
an unfading show of northern lights, what you, you asshole,
might call *aurora borealis*.
So sit down on the bed with my wife and me.
Faithful amanuensis, you can write down my last words,
not that they're great but maybe they are.
You wouldn't know. You're an *aurora borealis*.
But my wife is laughing and you're laughing too.
Just as we were at the beginning, just as we are at the end."

FUNKY STUFF

For a dead guy you looked pretty good,
because not only was your t-shirt clean
and you'd lost some weight but your faded tattoo
had been brightened beyond newness, restored
like the Sistine Chapel, and the acne divots
along your neck and cheek had been filled in
and even the deoxygenated liver color
of your skin had pinked up, so I thought
maybe the afterlife, which you never believed in,
was like purgatory, a place you got your body
ready for the limbo party of paradise,
but because this was a dream,
we were in a high-ceilinged attic, and you
who had never hoarded anything had filled
the space with piles of clothes, magazines
and newspapers stacked like pillars,
columns of books still in their shrink-wrap.
Here and there were clumps of rubber gloves—
black, orange, lavender, and yellow—for what
you called "the funky stuff." I asked, "What's
the funky stuff?" And you said, "I don't know,
but no one wants to touch it."

TO ISABELLA FRANCONATI

After your husband died and the cypress trees,
which he described as feathers constituting
"an evidence or inclination of God's breath,"
were cut down and milled into cigar boxes,
you closed the heavy blue shutters of his workroom
for the last time, the view unbearable that framed
his decades of silence in which he saw
in the brown river below, winding through its shallow
alluvial valley, the intractable force of his lost conviction,
reading as he did in everything formulations of soul and spirit.

To live as long as you did in the shadow of a man no longer
casting a shadow brought forth a light from you
that outshone his solitude and dispelled
your nostalgia for his former intensities.

That's why you would not countenance
acolytes, like me, whose reverence for the time and place
of his self-making forgave what you, suffering
his dissolution, could not forgive, a man who broke
faith with all the tenets he'd devised for art
and whose failure in life, the hollowness of his days,
was another way for us to assume safely the peril
of his vocation.
                    Unlike you, we began in disbelief
and so to be given faith, even an empty one, was a gift.

"After death," he wrote, "there are two alternatives,
both heartless: memory & forgetfulness."

                    Franconati
was a made-up name and you, his friend, Isabella,
were a made-up wife.

                I loved one of you before I loved you both.

        Memory or forgetfulness?

                        In the long posthumous life
he bequeathed us, which came first?

✳ ✳ ✳

BRONZE FOOT IN A GLASS CASE

In a museum

Basra is a long way off. I walked there once,
along the Euphrates. When I say, "I,"
I mean this foot without a leg to lift it.
Step by step I marched.

After Basra, I returned to Palmyra,
"City of Palms," and stood
a century or two in the shadow
of a wall, a foot with hundreds of feet] ?

waiting for men of flesh and blood
to flood the city with violence,
killing everything that walked,
everything with legs and arms and heads.

If you, who are bending close to me,
can look through the glare
of your own reflection, you'll see
the layer of dust at my heel

and the shadows my toes cast
on the baize. This is where
the waiting ends, this is where
the violence recommences—

in the dust and light   who? Audience? The poet themselves?
that gathers around me—you
who could not see it   the violence? the dust?
until I told you to look.

79

"Jefferson's Bees" is in memory of Philip Levine.

"Len Bias, a Bouquet of Flowers, and Ms. Brooks": The end words are taken from lines 5 and 6 of Gwendolyn Brooks's "The Last Quatrain of the Ballad of Emmett Till": "She kisses her killed boy. / And she is sorry." Len Bias, a University of Maryland basketball player, died of a drug overdose shortly after being drafted by the Boston Celtics.

"Koi" is in memory of Carol Houck Smith.

"Boom Boom" responds to Pablo Neruda's "Infancia y poesía" in *Obras Completas*, Vol. 1, 3rd ed. (Buenos Aires: Losada, 1967), 34.

"My Bishop": http://www.nytimes.com/2003/06/17/us/phoenix-bishop-arrested-in-fatal-hit-and-run-accident.html.

"The Storm" quotes lines 11 through 17 of John Berryman's "Winter Landscape," from *John Berryman: Collected Poems, 1937–1971*, edited and introduced by Charles Thornbury (New York: Farrar, Straus & Giroux, 1989).

"To Isabella Franconati" is in memory of Jon Anderson. Franconati and Isabella Franconati are literary inventions found in the poems of Jon Anderson and Steve Orlen.

"Bronze Foot in a Glass Case" is displayed in the National Museum of Damascus.

Made in the USA
San Bernardino, CA
08 March 2019